50 Persian Stew Recipes for Home

By: Kelly Johnson

Table of Contents

- Ghormeh Sabzi
- Fesenjan
- Gheimeh
- Bademjan Stew
- Khoresht-e Karafs
- Khoresht-e Beh
- Khoresht-e Bamieh
- Khoresht-e Kadoo
- Khoresht-e Aloo Esfenaj
- Khoresht-e Havij
- Khoresht-e Adas
- Khoresht-e Loobia
- Khoresht-e Nokhod
- Khoresht-e Sabzi (Herb Stew)
- Khoresht-e Morgh
- Khoresht-e Kalam
- Khoresht-e Gondi
- Khoresht-e Mast O Khiar
- Khoresht-e Sib
- Khoresht-e Shalgham
- Khoresht-e Havij Polo
- Khoresht-e Kadoo Polo
- Khoresht-e Baghali Polo
- Khoresht-e Gheymeh Polo
- Khoresht-e Zereshk Polo
- Khoresht-e Morgh Polo
- Khoresht-e Albaloo Polo
- Khoresht-e Adas Polo
- Khoresht-e Loobia Polo
- Khoresht-e Kalam Polo
- Khoresht-e Bademjan Polo
- Khoresht-e Fesenjan Polo
- Khoresht-e Sabzi Polo Ba Mahicheh
- Khoresht-e Sib Polo
- Khoresht-e Nargesi

- Khoresht-e Havij Ba Morgh
- Khoresht-e Torsh
- Khoresht-e Kadoo Ba Morgh
- Khoresht-e Khorma
- Khoresht-e Havij Polo Ba Mahicheh
- Khoresht-e Havij Ba Gosht
- Khoresht-e Gheymeh Polo Ba Mahicheh
- Khoresht-e Kalam Polo Ba Mahicheh
- Khoresht-e Khoresheh
- Khoresht-e Baghali Polo Ba Mahicheh
- Khoresht-e Morgh Polo Ba Mahicheh
- Khoresht-e Adas Polo Ba Mahicheh
- Khoresht-e Loobia Polo Ba Mahicheh
- Khoresht-e Zereshk Polo Ba Mahicheh
- Khoresht-e Sib Polo Ba Mahicheh

Ghormeh Sabzi

- Ingredients:
    - Diced lamb or beef
    - A mix of fresh herbs (parsley, cilantro, fenugreek, and green onions)
    - Dried fenugreek leaves (shanbalileh)
    - Red kidney beans
    - Dried Persian limes (limoo amani)
    - Onion
    - Turmeric, salt, and pepper
    - Oil for frying
- Instructions:
    - Saute diced onions in oil until golden brown.
    - Add meat and brown it on all sides.
    - Incorporate chopped herbs and let them cook down.
    - Add dried fenugreek leaves, turmeric, salt, and pepper for seasoning.
    - Pour in enough water to cover the ingredients, and bring to a boil.
    - Add red kidney beans and dried Persian limes.
    - Simmer until the meat is tender and the flavors meld together.
    - Serve Ghormeh Sabzi over rice.

This stew is a delightful blend of savory and tangy flavors, showcasing the rich culinary tradition of Persian cuisine.

Fesenjan

- Ingredients:
    - Chicken or duck pieces
    - Ground walnuts
    - Pomegranate molasses
    - Onion
    - Vegetable oil
    - Turmeric, salt, and pepper
    - Sugar (optional)
- Instructions:
    - Sauté finely chopped onions in oil until golden brown.
    - Add turmeric, salt, and pepper to the onions.
    - Incorporate ground walnuts, stirring to create a thick paste.
    - Add pomegranate molasses and continue stirring.
    - Place chicken or duck pieces into the mixture, coating them well.
    - Pour in enough water to cover the ingredients, bring to a boil, then simmer until the meat is cooked.
    - Optionally, add sugar to balance the tartness of the pomegranate molasses.
    - Simmer until the stew reaches a rich, velvety consistency.

Fesenjan is often served over rice, providing a delightful harmony of nutty, sweet, and tangy flavors that make it a cherished dish in Persian cuisine.

Gheimeh

- Ingredients:
    - Diced lamb or beef
    - Yellow split peas
    - Onion
    - Tomato paste
    - Dried limes (limoo amani)
    - Turmeric, cinnamon, salt, and pepper
    - Cooking oil
- Instructions:
    - Sauté finely chopped onions in oil until golden.
    - Add diced meat, turmeric, salt, and pepper, browning the meat on all sides.
    - Mix in yellow split peas, stirring to coat them with the spices.
    - Add tomato paste and continue stirring to combine.
    - Pour in enough water to cover the ingredients, bring to a boil, then reduce heat to simmer.
    - Add dried limes to the stew, creating a tangy flavor.
    - Allow the stew to simmer until the meat is tender and the split peas are cooked.
    - Adjust seasoning if needed and serve Gheimeh over rice.

Gheimeh is known for its hearty and comforting nature, with the dried limes imparting a distinctive citrusy note to the dish. It's a cherished part of Persian cuisine.

Bademjan Stew

- Ingredients:
    Eggplants (aubergines)
    Diced lamb or beef
    Onion
    Tomato paste
    Crushed tomatoes
    Turmeric, salt, and pepper
    Cooking oil
- Instructions:
    Cut eggplants into slices or cubes and soak them in salted water to reduce bitterness.
    Sauté finely chopped onions in oil until golden.
    Add diced meat, turmeric, salt, and pepper, browning the meat on all sides.
    Incorporate tomato paste, stirring to coat the meat and onions.
    Add crushed tomatoes to create a rich base for the stew.
    Rinse and drain the soaked eggplants, then add them to the pot.
    Pour in enough water to cover the ingredients, bring to a boil, then simmer until the meat is tender and the eggplants are cooked.
    Adjust seasoning if needed and serve Bademjan Stew over rice.

This dish showcases the delicious combination of savory meat, tender eggplants, and a tomato-based sauce, making it a delightful and comforting part of Persian cuisine.

Khoresht-e Karafs

- Ingredients:
    - Stewing meat (lamb or beef), cut into cubes
    - Celery, chopped
    - Onion, finely chopped
    - Diced tomatoes or tomato paste
    - Dried mint
    - Turmeric, salt, and pepper
    - Cooking oil
- Instructions:
    - Sauté finely chopped onions in oil until golden.
    - Add the cubed meat, turmeric, salt, and pepper, browning the meat on all sides.
    - Incorporate diced tomatoes or tomato paste, stirring to create a base for the stew.
    - Add chopped celery to the pot.
    - Pour in enough water to cover the ingredients, bring to a boil, then simmer until the meat is tender and the celery is cooked.
    - Sprinkle dried mint into the stew for added flavor.
    - Adjust seasoning if needed and serve Khoresht-e Karafs over rice.

Khoresht-e Karafs offers a unique blend of flavors with the earthy taste of celery complementing the savory meat and aromatic spices, making it a distinctive dish in Persian cuisine.

Khoresht-e Beh

- Ingredients:
    - Quince, peeled, cored, and sliced
    - Stewing meat (lamb or beef), cut into cubes
    - Onion, finely chopped
    - Tomato paste
    - Dried lime (limoo amani), pierced
    - Turmeric, cinnamon, salt, and pepper
    - Cooking oil
- Instructions:
    - Sauté finely chopped onions in oil until golden.
    - Add the cubed meat, turmeric, salt, and pepper, browning the meat on all sides.
    - Stir in tomato paste, creating a base for the stew.
    - Add sliced quince to the pot.
    - Pour in enough water to cover the ingredients, bring to a boil, then reduce heat to simmer.
    - Place a pierced dried lime into the stew to impart a tangy flavor.
    - Simmer until the meat is tender and the quince is soft.
    - Adjust seasoning if needed and serve Khoresht-e Beh over rice.

This dish showcases the unique combination of sweet quince, savory meat, and aromatic spices, creating a delightful and flavorful stew in Persian cuisine.

Khoresht-e Bamieh

Ingredients:

- Okra, whole or sliced
- Stewing meat (lamb or beef), cut into cubes
- Onion, finely chopped
- Tomatoes, chopped or tomato paste
- Garlic, minced
- Turmeric, salt, and pepper
- Cooking oil

Instructions:

Sauté finely chopped onions and minced garlic in oil until golden.
Add the cubed meat, turmeric, salt, and pepper, browning the meat on all sides.
Stir in chopped tomatoes or tomato paste to create a base for the stew.
Add the okra to the pot, ensuring it's well-coated with the tomato mixture.
Pour in enough water to cover the ingredients, bring to a boil, then reduce heat to simmer.
Simmer until the meat is tender and the okra is cooked through.
Adjust seasoning if needed.

Khoresht-e Bamieh is typically served over rice and showcases the unique texture and flavor of okra within the savory tomato and meat stew.

Khoresht-e Kadoo

Ingredients:

- Zucchini (kadoo), sliced
- Stewing meat (lamb or beef), cut into cubes
- Onion, finely chopped
- Tomatoes, chopped or tomato paste
- Turmeric, cinnamon, salt, and pepper
- Cooking oil

Instructions:

Sauté finely chopped onions in oil until golden.
Add the cubed meat, turmeric, salt, and pepper, browning the meat on all sides.
Stir in chopped tomatoes or tomato paste to create a base for the stew.
Add the sliced zucchini to the pot, ensuring it's well-coated with the tomato mixture.
Pour in enough water to cover the ingredients, bring to a boil, then reduce heat to simmer.
Sprinkle cinnamon for additional aromatic notes.
Simmer until the meat is tender, and the zucchini is cooked through.
Adjust seasoning if needed and serve Khoresht-e Kadoo over rice.

This dish highlights the tender texture of zucchini combined with savory meat and aromatic spices, creating a delicious and comforting stew in Persian cuisine.

Khoresht-e Aloo Esfenaj

Ingredients:

- Stewing meat (lamb or beef), cut into cubes
- Potatoes, peeled and cubed
- Fresh spinach, washed and chopped
- Onion, finely chopped
- Tomatoes, chopped or tomato paste
- Turmeric, salt, and pepper
- Cooking oil

Instructions:

Sauté finely chopped onions in oil until golden.
Add the cubed meat, turmeric, salt, and pepper, browning the meat on all sides.
Stir in chopped tomatoes or tomato paste to create a base for the stew.
Add the cubed potatoes to the pot.
Pour in enough water to cover the ingredients, bring to a boil, then reduce heat to simmer.
Add the chopped fresh spinach to the pot.
Simmer until the meat is tender, the potatoes are cooked, and the spinach is wilted.
Adjust seasoning if needed and serve Khoresht-e Aloo Esfenaj over rice.

This dish combines the heartiness of potatoes with the nutritious and vibrant flavors of spinach, creating a well-balanced stew in Persian cuisine.

Khoresht-e Havij

Ingredients:

- Stewing meat (lamb or beef), cut into cubes
- Carrots, peeled and sliced
- Onion, finely chopped
- Tomatoes, chopped or tomato paste
- Turmeric, cinnamon, salt, and pepper
- Cooking oil

Instructions:

Sauté finely chopped onions in oil until golden.
Add the cubed meat, turmeric, salt, and pepper, browning the meat on all sides.
Stir in chopped tomatoes or tomato paste to create a base for the stew.
Add the sliced carrots to the pot.
Pour in enough water to cover the ingredients, bring to a boil, then reduce heat to simmer.
Sprinkle cinnamon for additional aromatic notes.
Simmer until the meat is tender, and the carrots are cooked through.
Adjust seasoning if needed and serve Khoresht-e Havij over rice.

Khoresht-e Havij offers a delightful combination of sweet carrots and savory meat, creating a comforting and flavorful stew in Persian cuisine.

Khoresht-e Adas

Ingredients:

- Red or brown lentils, washed
- Onion, finely chopped
- Stewing meat (lamb or beef), cut into cubes (optional)
- Tomato paste or chopped tomatoes
- Turmeric, cumin, salt, and pepper
- Cooking oil

Instructions:

Sauté finely chopped onions in oil until golden.
If using meat, add the cubed meat, turmeric, salt, and pepper, browning the meat on all sides.
Stir in tomato paste or chopped tomatoes to create a base for the stew.
Add washed lentils to the pot.
Pour in enough water to cover the ingredients, bring to a boil, then reduce heat to simmer.
Season with cumin for additional flavor.
Simmer until the lentils are cooked through and the stew reaches a desired consistency.
Adjust seasoning if needed.

Khoresht-e Adas is often served over rice and provides a wholesome combination of protein from lentils and meat, along with the aromatic spices that characterize Persian cuisine.

Khoresht-e Loobia

Ingredients:

- Green beans (fresh or frozen), trimmed and chopped
- Stewing meat (lamb or beef), cut into cubes
- Onion, finely chopped
- Tomatoes, chopped or tomato paste
- Turmeric, cinnamon, salt, and pepper
- Cooking oil

Instructions:

Sauté finely chopped onions in oil until golden.
Add the cubed meat, turmeric, salt, and pepper, browning the meat on all sides.
Stir in chopped tomatoes or tomato paste to create a base for the stew.
Add the chopped green beans to the pot.
Pour in enough water to cover the ingredients, bring to a boil, then reduce heat to simmer.
Sprinkle cinnamon for additional aromatic notes.
Simmer until the meat is tender, and the green beans are cooked through.
Adjust seasoning if needed and serve Khoresht-e Loobia over rice.

Khoresht-e Loobia offers a combination of the crisp texture of green beans with savory meat, creating a delicious and balanced stew in Persian cuisine.

Khoresht-e Nokhod

Ingredients:

- Chickpeas (dried and soaked overnight, or canned and drained)
- Stewing meat (lamb or beef), cut into cubes
- Onion, finely chopped
- Tomatoes, chopped or tomato paste
- Turmeric, cinnamon, ground cumin, salt, and pepper
- Cooking oil

Instructions:

If using dried chickpeas, soak them overnight and cook until tender. If using canned chickpeas, drain and rinse them.
Sauté finely chopped onions in oil until golden.
Add the cubed meat, turmeric, salt, and pepper, browning the meat on all sides.
Stir in chopped tomatoes or tomato paste to create a base for the stew.
Add the cooked or canned chickpeas to the pot.
Pour in enough water to cover the ingredients, bring to a boil, then reduce heat to simmer.
Add ground cumin and cinnamon for additional flavor.
Simmer until the meat is tender, and the chickpeas are well incorporated into the stew.
Adjust seasoning if needed and serve Khoresht-e Nokhod over rice.

Khoresht-e Nokhod provides a hearty and nutritious dish, combining the protein-rich chickpeas with savory meat and aromatic spices, as is characteristic of Persian cuisine.

Khoresht-e Sabzi (Herb Stew)

Ingredients:

- A mix of fresh herbs (parsley, cilantro, dill, and green onions), finely chopped
- Stewing meat (lamb or beef), cut into cubes
- Dried fenugreek leaves (shanbalileh)
- Red kidney beans (precooked or canned)
- Onion, finely chopped
- Garlic, minced
- Dried Persian limes (limoo amani), pierced
- Turmeric, salt, and pepper
- Cooking oil

Instructions:

Sauté finely chopped onions and minced garlic in oil until golden.
Add the cubed meat, turmeric, salt, and pepper, browning the meat on all sides.
Stir in the chopped fresh herbs and dried fenugreek leaves.
Add the red kidney beans to the pot.
Pour in enough water to cover the ingredients, bring to a boil, then reduce heat to simmer.
Place the pierced dried Persian limes into the stew.
Simmer until the meat is tender, and the herbs are well incorporated into the stew.

Sabzi Polo (Herbed Rice):

For Sabzi Polo, you would separately prepare herbed rice by mixing Basmati rice with a combination of finely chopped herbs such as parsley, cilantro, dill, and green onions. Cook the rice with salt and turmeric, creating a fragrant and colorful dish.

Serve Khoresht-e Sabzi over the Sabzi Polo rice for a traditional and delicious Persian meal. Adjust seasoning as needed and enjoy!

Khoresht-e Morgh

Ingredients:

- Chicken pieces (whole chicken or parts like thighs and drumsticks)
- Onion, finely chopped
- Tomatoes, chopped or tomato paste
- Dried Persian limes (limoo amani), pierced
- Saffron threads (optional)
- Turmeric, cinnamon, salt, and pepper
- Cooking oil

Instructions:

Sauté finely chopped onions in oil until golden.
Add the chicken pieces, turmeric, salt, and pepper, browning the chicken on all sides.
Stir in chopped tomatoes or tomato paste to create a base for the stew.
Place the pierced dried Persian limes into the stew.
If using saffron, dissolve it in a bit of warm water and add it to the stew for color and flavor.
Pour in enough water to cover the ingredients, bring to a boil, then reduce heat to simmer.
Add cinnamon for additional aromatic notes.
Simmer until the chicken is cooked through, and the stew reaches a desired consistency.
Adjust seasoning if needed.

Khoresht-e Morgh is often served over rice and provides a delightful combination of tender chicken infused with Persian spices.

Khoresht-e Kalam

Ingredients:

- Cabbage, chopped
- Stewing meat (lamb or beef), cut into cubes
- Onion, finely chopped
- Tomatoes, chopped or tomato paste
- Turmeric, cinnamon, salt, and pepper
- Cooking oil

Instructions:

Sauté finely chopped onions in oil until golden.
Add the cubed meat, turmeric, salt, and pepper, browning the meat on all sides.
Stir in chopped tomatoes or tomato paste to create a base for the stew.
Add the chopped cabbage to the pot.
Pour in enough water to cover the ingredients, bring to a boil, then reduce heat to simmer.
Sprinkle cinnamon for additional aromatic notes.
Simmer until the meat is tender, and the cabbage is cooked through.
Adjust seasoning if needed and serve Khoresht-e Kalam over rice.

Khoresht-e Kalam offers a combination of the slightly sweet and earthy flavor of cabbage with savory meat, creating a delicious and comforting stew in Persian cuisine.

Khoresht-e Gondi

Ingredients:

- Chicken meatballs (Gondi)
- Onion, finely chopped
- Dried Persian limes (limoo amani), pierced
- Turmeric, cinnamon, salt, and pepper
- Chickpeas (precooked or canned)
- Cooking oil

Instructions:

Sauté finely chopped onions in oil until golden.
Add the pre-cooked chicken meatballs, turmeric, salt, and pepper, browning them a bit.
Place the pierced dried Persian limes into the stew.
Add pre-cooked chickpeas to the pot.
Pour in enough water to cover the ingredients, bring to a boil, then reduce heat to simmer.
Sprinkle cinnamon for additional aromatic notes.
Simmer until the flavors meld together, and the stew reaches a desired consistency.
Adjust seasoning if needed and serve Khoresht-e Gondi over rice.

Khoresht-e Gondi showcases the unique texture and flavor of the chicken meatballs in a delicious Persian stew.

Khoresht-e Mast O Khiar

Ingredients:

- Plain yogurt
- Cucumbers, peeled and diced
- Fresh mint, finely chopped
- Fresh dill, finely chopped
- Garlic, minced
- Salt and pepper to taste
- Dried mint (for garnish)
- Ice cubes (optional)

Instructions:

In a bowl, combine plain yogurt with diced cucumbers, chopped mint, chopped dill, and minced garlic.

Mix well until the ingredients are evenly distributed.

Season the mixture with salt and pepper to taste.

If desired, add ice cubes to the mixture for a chilled version.

Garnish with a sprinkle of dried mint on top.

Serve immediately or refrigerate before serving.

Khoresht-e Mast o Khiar is often served as a side dish or appetizer and is especially popular during hot weather due to its cooling and refreshing nature. It's a delightful addition to a Persian meal.

Khoresht-e Sib

Ingredients:

- Stewing meat (lamb or beef), cut into cubes
- Apples, peeled, cored, and sliced
- Onion, finely chopped
- Tomatoes, chopped or tomato paste
- Turmeric, cinnamon, salt, and pepper
- Cooking oil

Instructions:

Sauté finely chopped onions in oil until golden.
Add the cubed meat, turmeric, salt, and pepper, browning the meat on all sides.
Stir in chopped tomatoes or tomato paste to create a base for the stew.
Add the sliced apples to the pot.
Pour in enough water to cover the ingredients, bring to a boil, then reduce heat to simmer.
Sprinkle cinnamon for additional aromatic notes.
Simmer until the meat is tender, and the apples are cooked through.
Adjust seasoning if needed and serve Khoresht-e Sib over rice.

Khoresht-e Sib offers a unique combination of savory meat with the sweetness of apples, creating a delicious and comforting stew in Persian cuisine.

Khoresht-e Shalgham

Ingredients:

- Stewing meat (lamb or beef), cut into cubes
- Turnips, peeled and sliced
- Onion, finely chopped
- Tomatoes, chopped or tomato paste
- Turmeric, cinnamon, salt, and pepper
- Cooking oil

Instructions:

Sauté finely chopped onions in oil until golden.
Add the cubed meat, turmeric, salt, and pepper, browning the meat on all sides.
Stir in chopped tomatoes or tomato paste to create a base for the stew.
Add the sliced turnips to the pot.
Pour in enough water to cover the ingredients, bring to a boil, then reduce heat to simmer.
Sprinkle cinnamon for additional aromatic notes.
Simmer until the meat is tender, and the turnips are cooked through.
Adjust seasoning if needed and serve Khoresht-e Shalgham over rice.

Khoresht-e Shalgham combines the earthy flavor of turnips with savory meat and aromatic spices, creating a delicious and comforting stew in Persian cuisine.

Khoresht-e Havij Polo

Ingredients:

For the Carrot Stew (Khoresht-e Havij):

- Stewing meat (lamb or beef), cut into cubes
- Carrots, peeled and sliced
- Onion, finely chopped
- Tomatoes, chopped or tomato paste
- Turmeric, cinnamon, salt, and pepper
- Cooking oil

For the Aromatic Rice (Polo):

- Basmati rice
- Saffron threads (optional, for coloring)
- Butter or cooking oil

Instructions:

Khoresht-e Havij (Carrot Stew):

Sauté finely chopped onions in oil until golden.
Add the cubed meat, turmeric, salt, and pepper, browning the meat on all sides.
Stir in chopped tomatoes or tomato paste to create a base for the stew.
Add the sliced carrots to the pot.
Pour in enough water to cover the ingredients, bring to a boil, then reduce heat to simmer.
Sprinkle cinnamon for additional aromatic notes.
Simmer until the meat is tender, and the carrots are cooked through.
Adjust seasoning if needed.

Aromatic Rice (Polo):

Rinse the Basmati rice thoroughly.

In a separate pot, bring water to a boil, add salt, and cook the rice until it's parboiled (half-cooked).

Drain the rice and set aside.

If using saffron, dissolve it in a bit of warm water.

In the pot, layer the partially cooked rice with saffron and butter or oil.

Wrap the pot lid with a clean kitchen towel to absorb steam.

Cook the rice over low heat until it's fully cooked and has developed a crispy layer at the bottom.

Serve the Khoresht-e Havij over the aromatic Polo, and enjoy this delicious and aromatic Persian dish. Adjust seasoning if needed.

Khoresht-e Kadoo Polo

Ingredients:

For the Zucchini Stew (Khoresht-e Kadoo):

- Zucchini (kadoo), sliced
- Stewing meat (lamb or beef), cut into cubes
- Onion, finely chopped
- Tomatoes, chopped or tomato paste
- Turmeric, cinnamon, salt, and pepper
- Cooking oil

For the Aromatic Rice (Polo):

- Basmati rice
- Saffron threads (optional, for coloring)
- Butter or cooking oil

Instructions:

Khoresht-e Kadoo (Zucchini Stew):

    Sauté finely chopped onions in oil until golden.
    Add the cubed meat, turmeric, salt, and pepper, browning the meat on all sides.
    Stir in chopped tomatoes or tomato paste to create a base for the stew.
    Add the sliced zucchini to the pot.
    Pour in enough water to cover the ingredients, bring to a boil, then reduce heat to simmer.
    Sprinkle cinnamon for additional aromatic notes.
    Simmer until the meat is tender, and the zucchini is cooked through.
    Adjust seasoning if needed.

Aromatic Rice (Polo):

    Rinse the Basmati rice thoroughly.
    In a separate pot, bring water to a boil, add salt, and cook the rice until it's parboiled (half-cooked).
    Drain the rice and set aside.
    If using saffron, dissolve it in a bit of warm water.

In the pot, layer the partially cooked rice with saffron and butter or oil.
Wrap the pot lid with a clean kitchen towel to absorb steam.
Cook the rice over low heat until it's fully cooked and has developed a crispy layer at the bottom.

Serve the Khoresht-e Kadoo over the aromatic Polo, and enjoy this delightful Persian dish. Adjust seasoning if needed.

Khoresht-e Baghali Polo

Ingredients:

For the Stew (Khoresht-e Baghali):

- Fava beans (fresh or frozen), shelled
- Lamb or beef, cut into cubes
- Onion, finely chopped
- Fresh dill, chopped
- Dried lime (limoo amani), pierced
- Turmeric, salt, and pepper
- Cooking oil

For the Aromatic Rice (Polo):

- Basmati rice
- Saffron threads (optional, for coloring)
- Butter or cooking oil

Instructions:

Khoresht-e Baghali (Fava Bean Stew):

Sauté finely chopped onions in oil until golden.
Add the cubed meat, turmeric, salt, and pepper, browning the meat on all sides.
Stir in the fava beans and chopped fresh dill.
Add the pierced dried lime to the pot.
Pour in enough water to cover the ingredients, bring to a boil, then reduce heat to simmer.
Simmer until the meat is tender, and the fava beans are cooked through.
Adjust seasoning if needed.

Aromatic Rice (Polo):

Rinse the Basmati rice thoroughly.
In a separate pot, bring water to a boil, add salt, and cook the rice until it's parboiled (half-cooked).
Drain the rice and set aside.
If using saffron, dissolve it in a bit of warm water.

In the pot, layer the partially cooked rice with saffron and butter or oil.
Wrap the pot lid with a clean kitchen towel to absorb steam.
Cook the rice over low heat until it's fully cooked and has developed a crispy layer at the bottom.

Serve the Khoresht-e Baghali over the aromatic Polo, and enjoy this classic Persian dish. Adjust seasoning if needed.

Khoresht-e Gheymeh Polo

Ingredients:

For the Gheymeh Stew:

- Yellow split peas, soaked and drained
- Lamb or beef, cut into cubes
- Onion, finely chopped
- Tomato paste
- Dried limes (limoo amani), pierced
- Turmeric, salt, and pepper
- Cooking oil

For the Aromatic Rice (Polo):

- Basmati rice
- Saffron threads (optional, for coloring)
- Butter or cooking oil

Instructions:

Gheymeh Stew:

- Sauté finely chopped onions in oil until golden.
- Add the cubed meat, turmeric, salt, and pepper, browning the meat on all sides.
- Add soaked and drained yellow split peas to the pot.
- Stir in tomato paste and continue to sauté.
- Add enough water to cover the ingredients, bring to a boil, then reduce heat to simmer.
- Add the pierced dried limes to the stew for a tangy flavor.
- Simmer until the meat is tender, and the split peas are cooked through.
- Adjust seasoning if needed.

Aromatic Rice (Polo):

- Rinse the Basmati rice thoroughly.
- In a separate pot, bring water to a boil, add salt, and cook the rice until it's parboiled (half-cooked).
- Drain the rice and set aside.

If using saffron, dissolve it in a bit of warm water.
In the pot, layer the partially cooked rice with saffron and butter or oil.
Wrap the pot lid with a clean kitchen towel to absorb steam.
Cook the rice over low heat until it's fully cooked and has developed a crispy layer at the bottom.

Serve the Gheymeh stew over the aromatic Polo, and enjoy this classic Persian dish. Adjust seasoning if needed.

Khoresht-e Zereshk Polo

Ingredients:

For the Zereshk Polo (Barberry Rice):

- Basmati rice
- Dried barberries (zereshk), soaked in water
- Saffron threads (optional, for coloring)
- Butter or cooking oil

For the Chicken Stew:

- Chicken pieces (whole chicken or parts like thighs and drumsticks)
- Onion, finely chopped
- Tomato paste
- Dried limes (limoo amani), pierced
- Turmeric, cinnamon, salt, and pepper
- Cooking oil

Instructions:

Zereshk Polo (Barberry Rice):

Rinse the Basmati rice thoroughly.
In a separate pot, bring water to a boil, add salt, and cook the rice until it's parboiled (half-cooked).
Drain the rice and set aside.
If using saffron, dissolve it in a bit of warm water.
In the pot, layer the partially cooked rice with saffron and butter or oil.
Add soaked barberries on top.
Wrap the pot lid with a clean kitchen towel to absorb steam.
Cook the rice over low heat until it's fully cooked and has developed a crispy layer at the bottom.

Chicken Stew:

Sauté finely chopped onions in oil until golden.
Add the chicken pieces, turmeric, salt, and pepper, browning the chicken on all sides.

Stir in tomato paste to create a base for the stew.
Add the pierced dried limes to the pot.
Pour in enough water to cover the ingredients, bring to a boil, then reduce heat to simmer.
Sprinkle cinnamon for additional aromatic notes.
Simmer until the chicken is cooked through, and the stew reaches a desired consistency.
Adjust seasoning if needed.

Serve the Chicken Stew over the Barberry Rice, and enjoy the vibrant flavors of Khoresht-e Zereshk Polo. Adjust seasoning if needed.

Khoresht-e Morgh Polo

For the Chicken Stew (Khoresht-e Morgh):

- Chicken pieces (whole chicken or parts like thighs and drumsticks)
- Onion, finely chopped
- Tomatoes, chopped or tomato paste
- Dried Persian limes (limoo amani), pierced
- Saffron threads (optional, for coloring)
- Turmeric, cinnamon, salt, and pepper
- Cooking oil

For the Aromatic Rice (Polo):

- Basmati rice
- Butter or cooking oil

Instructions:

- Sauté finely chopped onions in oil until golden.
- Add the chicken pieces, turmeric, salt, and pepper, browning the chicken on all sides.
- Stir in chopped tomatoes or tomato paste to create a base for the stew.
- Add the pierced dried Persian limes to the pot.
- Dissolve saffron in a bit of warm water and add to the stew.
- Sprinkle cinnamon for additional aromatic notes.
- Pour in enough water to cover the ingredients, bring to a boil, then reduce heat to simmer.
- Simmer until the chicken is cooked through, and the stew reaches a desired consistency.
- Adjust seasoning if needed.

For the Polo (Aromatic Rice), cook Basmati rice separately, and layer it with butter or oil. Serve the Khoresht-e Morgh over the aromatic Polo.

These dishes are typically served together, with the flavorful stew complementing the aromatic rice. Adjust seasoning as needed and enjoy these classic Persian recipes!

Khoresht-e Albaloo Polo

For the Chicken Stew (Khoresht-e Albaloo):

- Chicken pieces (whole chicken or parts like thighs and drumsticks)
- Onion, finely chopped
- Sour cherries (fresh or canned), pitted
- Sugar
- Saffron threads (optional, for coloring)
- Turmeric, cinnamon, salt, and pepper
- Cooking oil

For the Aromatic Rice (Polo):

- Basmati rice
- Butter or cooking oil

Instructions:

Chicken Stew (Khoresht-e Albaloo):

Sauté finely chopped onions in oil until golden.
Add the chicken pieces, turmeric, salt, and pepper, browning the chicken on all sides.
Stir in pitted sour cherries and add sugar for sweetness.
Dissolve saffron in a bit of warm water and add to the stew.
Sprinkle cinnamon for additional aromatic notes.
Pour in enough water to cover the ingredients, bring to a boil, then reduce heat to simmer.
Simmer until the chicken is cooked through, and the stew reaches a desired consistency.
Adjust seasoning if needed.

Aromatic Rice (Polo):

Rinse Basmati rice thoroughly.
In a separate pot, bring water to a boil, add salt, and cook the rice until it's parboiled (half-cooked).
Drain the rice and set aside.
If using saffron, dissolve it in a bit of warm water.

In the pot, layer the partially cooked rice with saffron and butter or oil.
Wrap the pot lid with a clean kitchen towel to absorb steam.
Cook the rice over low heat until it's fully cooked and has developed a crispy layer at the bottom.

Serve the Khoresht-e Albaloo over the aromatic Polo, and enjoy the sweet and savory flavors of this classic Persian dish. Adjust seasoning as needed.

Khoresht-e Adas Polo

For the Chicken Stew (Khoresht-e Albaloo):

- Chicken pieces (whole chicken or parts like thighs and drumsticks)
- Onion, finely chopped
- Sour cherries, pitted (fresh or canned)
- Saffron threads (optional, for coloring)
- Sugar
- Turmeric, cinnamon, salt, and pepper
- Cooking oil

For the Aromatic Rice (Polo):

- Basmati rice
- Butter or cooking oil

Instructions:

Sauté finely chopped onions in oil until golden.
Add the chicken pieces, turmeric, salt, and pepper, browning the chicken on all sides.
Add sour cherries to the pot and sauté for a few minutes.
Dissolve saffron in a bit of warm water and add to the stew.
Add sugar to balance the tartness of the cherries.
Pour in enough water to cover the ingredients, bring to a boil, then reduce heat to simmer.
Simmer until the chicken is cooked through, and the stew reaches a desired consistency.
Adjust seasoning if needed.

For the Polo (Aromatic Rice), cook Basmati rice separately and layer it with butter or oil. Serve the Khoresht-e Albaloo over the aromatic Polo.

Khoresht-e Adas Polo (Lentil Rice with Chicken Stew):

For the Chicken Stew (Khoresht-e Adas):

- Chicken pieces (whole chicken or parts like thighs and drumsticks)
- Onion, finely chopped

- Red or brown lentils, washed
- Saffron threads (optional, for coloring)
- Turmeric, cumin, salt, and pepper
- Cooking oil

For the Aromatic Rice (Polo):

- Basmati rice
- Butter or cooking oil

Instructions:

Sauté finely chopped onions in oil until golden.
Add the chicken pieces, turmeric, salt, and pepper, browning the chicken on all sides.
Add washed lentils to the pot.
Dissolve saffron in a bit of warm water and add to the stew.
Season with cumin for additional flavor.
Pour in enough water to cover the ingredients, bring to a boil, then reduce heat to simmer.
Simmer until the chicken is cooked through, and the lentils are tender.
Adjust seasoning if needed.

For the Polo (Aromatic Rice), cook Basmati rice separately and layer it with butter or oil. Serve the Khoresht-e Adas over the aromatic Polo.

These dishes are typically served together, with the stew complementing the aromatic rice. Adjust seasoning as needed and enjoy these classic Persian recipes!
Khoresht-e Loobia Polo

For the Meat Stew (Khoresht-e Loobia):

- Stewing meat (lamb or beef), cut into cubes
- Green beans, trimmed and chopped
- Onion, finely chopped
- Tomatoes, chopped or tomato paste
- Turmeric, cinnamon, salt, and pepper
- Cooking oil

For the Aromatic Rice (Polo):

- Basmati rice
- Saffron threads (optional, for coloring)
- Butter or cooking oil

Instructions:

Meat Stew (Khoresht-e Loobia):

   Sauté finely chopped onions in oil until golden.
   Add the cubed meat, turmeric, salt, and pepper, browning the meat on all sides.
   Stir in chopped tomatoes or tomato paste to create a base for the stew.
   Add the chopped green beans to the pot.
   Pour in enough water to cover the ingredients, bring to a boil, then reduce heat to simmer.
   Sprinkle cinnamon for additional aromatic notes.
   Simmer until the meat is tender, and the green beans are cooked through.
   Adjust seasoning if needed.

Aromatic Rice (Polo):

   Rinse the Basmati rice thoroughly.
   In a separate pot, bring water to a boil, add salt, and cook the rice until it's parboiled (half-cooked).
   Drain the rice and set aside.
   If using saffron, dissolve it in a bit of warm water.
   In the pot, layer the partially cooked rice with saffron and butter or oil.
   Wrap the pot lid with a clean kitchen towel to absorb steam.
   Cook the rice over low heat until it's fully cooked and has developed a crispy layer at the bottom.

Serve the Khoresht-e Loobia over the aromatic Polo for a delicious combination of meat, green beans, and flavorful rice. Adjust seasoning as needed and enjoy this classic Persian dish!

Khoresht-e Kalam Polo

For the Meat Stew (Khoresht-e Kalam):

- Stewing meat (lamb or beef), cut into cubes
- Cabbage, chopped
- Onion, finely chopped
- Tomatoes, chopped or tomato paste
- Turmeric, cinnamon, salt, and pepper
- Cooking oil

For the Aromatic Rice (Polo):

- Basmati rice
- Saffron threads (optional, for coloring)
- Butter or cooking oil

Instructions:

Meat Stew (Khoresht-e Kalam):

Sauté finely chopped onions in oil until golden.
Add the cubed meat, turmeric, salt, and pepper, browning the meat on all sides.
Stir in chopped tomatoes or tomato paste to create a base for the stew.
Add the chopped cabbage to the pot.
Pour in enough water to cover the ingredients, bring to a boil, then reduce heat to simmer.
Sprinkle cinnamon for additional aromatic notes.
Simmer until the meat is tender, and the cabbage is cooked through.
Adjust seasoning if needed.

Aromatic Rice (Polo):

Rinse the Basmati rice thoroughly.
In a separate pot, bring water to a boil, add salt, and cook the rice until it's parboiled (half-cooked).
Drain the rice and set aside.

If using saffron, dissolve it in a bit of warm water.
In the pot, layer the partially cooked rice with saffron and butter or oil.
Wrap the pot lid with a clean kitchen towel to absorb steam.
Cook the rice over low heat until it's fully cooked and has developed a crispy layer at the bottom.

Serve the Khoresht-e Kalam over the aromatic Polo for a delightful combination of meat, cabbage, and flavorful rice. Adjust seasoning as needed and enjoy this classic Persian dish!

Khoresht-e Bademjan Polo

For the Meat Stew (Khoresht-e Bademjan):

- Stewing meat (lamb or beef), cut into cubes
- Eggplants (aubergines), peeled and sliced
- Onion, finely chopped
- Tomatoes, chopped or tomato paste
- Turmeric, cinnamon, salt, and pepper
- Cooking oil

For the Aromatic Rice (Polo):

- Basmati rice
- Saffron threads (optional, for coloring)
- Butter or cooking oil

Instructions:

Meat Stew (Khoresht-e Bademjan):

Sauté finely chopped onions in oil until golden.
Add the cubed meat, turmeric, salt, and pepper, browning the meat on all sides.
Stir in chopped tomatoes or tomato paste to create a base for the stew.
Add the sliced eggplants to the pot.
Pour in enough water to cover the ingredients, bring to a boil, then reduce heat to simmer.
Sprinkle cinnamon for additional aromatic notes.
Simmer until the meat is tender, and the eggplants are cooked through.
Adjust seasoning if needed.

Aromatic Rice (Polo):

Rinse the Basmati rice thoroughly.
In a separate pot, bring water to a boil, add salt, and cook the rice until it's parboiled (half-cooked).
Drain the rice and set aside.
If using saffron, dissolve it in a bit of warm water.
In the pot, layer the partially cooked rice with saffron and butter or oil.
Wrap the pot lid with a clean kitchen towel to absorb steam.

Cook the rice over low heat until it's fully cooked and has developed a crispy layer at the bottom.

Serve the Khoresht-e Bademjan over the aromatic Polo for a delicious combination of meat, eggplants, and flavorful rice. Adjust seasoning as needed and enjoy this classic Persian dish!

Khoresht-e Fesenjan Polo

For the Meat Stew (Khoresht-e Fesenjan):

- Stewing meat (chicken, lamb, or beef), cut into cubes
- Onion, finely chopped
- Pomegranate paste or molasses
- Ground walnuts
- Sugar
- Ground cinnamon
- Turmeric, salt, and pepper
- Cooking oil

For the Aromatic Rice (Polo):

- Basmati rice
- Saffron threads (optional, for coloring)
- Butter or cooking oil

Instructions:

Meat Stew (Khoresht-e Fesenjan):

Sauté finely chopped onions in oil until golden.
Add the cubed meat, turmeric, salt, and pepper, browning the meat on all sides.
Add ground walnuts to the pot and continue sautéing.
Stir in pomegranate paste or molasses, and sugar for sweetness.
Add ground cinnamon for additional flavor.
Pour in enough water to cover the ingredients, bring to a boil, then reduce heat to simmer.
Simmer until the meat is tender, and the stew reaches a desired consistency.
Adjust seasoning if needed.

Aromatic Rice (Polo):

Rinse the Basmati rice thoroughly.

In a separate pot, bring water to a boil, add salt, and cook the rice until it's parboiled (half-cooked).
Drain the rice and set aside.
If using saffron, dissolve it in a bit of warm water.
In the pot, layer the partially cooked rice with saffron and butter or oil.
Wrap the pot lid with a clean kitchen towel to absorb steam.
Cook the rice over low heat until it's fully cooked and has developed a crispy layer at the bottom.

Serve the Khoresht-e Fesenjan over the aromatic Polo for a rich and flavorful combination of meat, pomegranate, and walnut stew with delicious rice. Adjust seasoning as needed and enjoy this classic Persian dish!

Khoresht-e Sabzi Polo Ba Mahicheh

For the Lamb Shank Stew (Khoresht-e Sabzi Polo Ba Mahicheh):

- Lamb shanks
- A mix of fresh herbs (parsley, cilantro, dill, and green onions), finely chopped
- Fenugreek leaves (shanbalileh), dried
- Red kidney beans (precooked or canned)
- Onion, finely chopped
- Garlic, minced
- Dried Persian limes (limoo amani), pierced
- Turmeric, salt, and pepper
- Cooking oil

For the Aromatic Rice (Polo):

- Basmati rice
- Saffron threads (optional, for coloring)
- Butter or cooking oil

Instructions:

Lamb Shank Stew (Khoresht-e Sabzi Polo Ba Mahicheh):

Sauté finely chopped onions and minced garlic in oil until golden.
Add lamb shanks, turmeric, salt, and pepper, browning the meat on all sides.
Stir in the chopped fresh herbs and dried fenugreek leaves.
Add red kidney beans to the pot.
Pour in enough water to cover the ingredients, bring to a boil, then reduce heat to simmer.
Place the pierced dried Persian limes into the stew.
Simmer until the lamb shanks are tender and the herbs are well incorporated into the stew.
Adjust seasoning if needed.

Aromatic Rice (Polo):

Rinse the Basmati rice thoroughly.
In a separate pot, bring water to a boil, add salt, and cook the rice until it's parboiled (half-cooked).
Drain the rice and set aside.
If using saffron, dissolve it in a bit of warm water.
In the pot, layer the partially cooked rice with saffron and butter or oil.
Wrap the pot lid with a clean kitchen towel to absorb steam.
Cook the rice over low heat until it's fully cooked and has developed a crispy layer at the bottom.

Serve the Khoresht-e Sabzi Polo Ba Mahicheh by placing the lamb shanks on top of the aromatic Polo for a delicious and visually appealing presentation. Adjust seasoning as needed and enjoy this classic Persian dish!

Khoresht-e Sib Polo

For the Meat Stew (Khoresht-e Sib):

- Stewing meat (lamb or beef), cut into cubes
- Apples, peeled, cored, and sliced
- Onion, finely chopped
- Tomatoes, chopped or tomato paste
- Turmeric, cinnamon, salt, and pepper
- Cooking oil

For the Aromatic Rice (Polo):

- Basmati rice
- Saffron threads (optional, for coloring)
- Butter or cooking oil

Instructions:

Meat Stew (Khoresht-e Sib):

Sauté finely chopped onions in oil until golden.
Add the cubed meat, turmeric, salt, and pepper, browning the meat on all sides.
Stir in chopped tomatoes or tomato paste to create a base for the stew.
Add the sliced apples to the pot.
Pour in enough water to cover the ingredients, bring to a boil, then reduce heat to simmer.
Sprinkle cinnamon for additional aromatic notes.
Simmer until the meat is tender, and the apples are cooked through.
Adjust seasoning if needed.

Aromatic Rice (Polo):

Rinse the Basmati rice thoroughly.
In a separate pot, bring water to a boil, add salt, and cook the rice until it's parboiled (half-cooked).
Drain the rice and set aside.
If using saffron, dissolve it in a bit of warm water.
In the pot, layer the partially cooked rice with saffron and butter or oil.
Wrap the pot lid with a clean kitchen towel to absorb steam.

Cook the rice over low heat until it's fully cooked and has developed a crispy layer at the bottom.

Serve the Khoresht-e Sib over the aromatic Polo for a delightful combination of meat, apples, and flavorful rice. Adjust seasoning as needed and enjoy this classic Persian dish!

Khoresht-e Nargesi

Ingredients:

- Spinach, chopped
- Onion, finely chopped
- Garlic, minced
- Stewing meat (lamb or beef), cut into cubes (optional)
- Turmeric, salt, and pepper
- Cooking oil

Instructions:

In a pot, sauté finely chopped onions in oil until golden.
If using meat, add the cubed meat, turmeric, salt, and pepper. Brown the meat on all sides.
Stir in minced garlic and sauté for a minute until fragrant.
Add the chopped spinach to the pot.
Pour in enough water to cover the ingredients, bring to a boil, then reduce heat to simmer.
Simmer until the spinach is cooked through and the flavors meld together.
Adjust seasoning if needed.

Serve Khoresht-e Nargesi over rice or with flatbread. It's a simple and delicious Persian spinach stew that can be enjoyed on its own or as a side dish. Adjust the quantities based on the number of servings you need.

Khoresht-e Havij Ba Morgh

Ingredients:

- Chicken pieces (whole chicken or parts like thighs and drumsticks)
- Carrots, peeled and sliced
- Onion, finely chopped
- Tomatoes, chopped or tomato paste
- Turmeric, cinnamon, salt, and pepper
- Cooking oil

Instructions:

> Sauté finely chopped onions in oil until golden.
> Add the chicken pieces, turmeric, salt, and pepper, browning the chicken on all sides.
> Stir in chopped tomatoes or tomato paste to create a base for the stew.
> Add the sliced carrots to the pot.
> Pour in enough water to cover the ingredients, bring to a boil, then reduce heat to simmer.
> Sprinkle cinnamon for additional aromatic notes.
> Simmer until the chicken is cooked through, and the carrots are tender.
> Adjust seasoning if needed.

Serve Khoresht-e Havij Ba Morgh over rice or with flatbread. It's a flavorful and comforting Persian dish combining the sweetness of carrots with the savory taste of chicken. Adjust the quantities based on the number of servings you need.

Khoresht-e Torsh

Ingredients:

- Stewing meat (lamb or beef), cut into cubes
- Onions, finely chopped
- Dried sour fruits (plums, apricots, or sour cherries)
- Pomegranate paste or molasses
- Walnuts, ground
- Turmeric, cinnamon, salt, and pepper
- Cooking oil

Instructions:

Sauté finely chopped onions in oil until golden.
Add the cubed meat, turmeric, salt, and pepper, browning the meat on all sides.
Add dried sour fruits to the pot.
Stir in ground walnuts and pomegranate paste or molasses.
Pour in enough water to cover the ingredients, bring to a boil, then reduce heat to simmer.
Sprinkle cinnamon for additional aromatic notes.
Simmer until the meat is tender, and the stew reaches a desired consistency.
Adjust seasoning if needed.

Serve Khoresht-e Torsh over rice. This Persian sour stew combines the tanginess of sour fruits and pomegranate with the richness of meat, creating a unique and delicious flavor. Adjust the quantities based on the number of servings you need.

Khoresht-e Kadoo Ba Morgh

Ingredients:

- Chicken pieces (whole chicken or parts like thighs and drumsticks)
- Zucchini, sliced
- Onion, finely chopped
- Tomatoes, chopped or tomato paste
- Turmeric, cinnamon, salt, and pepper
- Cooking oil

Instructions:

Sauté finely chopped onions in oil until golden.
Add the chicken pieces, turmeric, salt, and pepper, browning the chicken on all sides.
Stir in chopped tomatoes or tomato paste to create a base for the stew.
Add the sliced zucchini to the pot.
Pour in enough water to cover the ingredients, bring to a boil, then reduce heat to simmer.
Sprinkle cinnamon for additional aromatic notes.
Simmer until the chicken is cooked through, and the zucchini is tender.
Adjust seasoning if needed.

Serve Khoresht-e Kadoo Ba Morgh over rice or with flatbread. This Persian stew combines the succulence of chicken with the mild flavor of zucchini for a delicious and comforting dish. Adjust the quantities based on the number of servings you need.

Khoresht-e Khorma

Ingredients:

- Stewing meat (lamb or beef), cut into cubes
- Dates, pitted and chopped
- Onion, finely chopped
- Tomato paste
- Turmeric, cinnamon, salt, and pepper
- Cooking oil

Instructions:

- Sauté finely chopped onions in oil until golden.
- Add the cubed meat, turmeric, salt, and pepper, browning the meat on all sides.
- Stir in tomato paste to create a base for the stew.
- Add the chopped dates to the pot.
- Pour in enough water to cover the ingredients, bring to a boil, then reduce heat to simmer.
- Sprinkle cinnamon for additional aromatic notes.
- Simmer until the meat is tender, and the stew reaches a desired consistency.
- Adjust seasoning if needed.

Serve Khoresht-e Khorma over rice or with flatbread. This Persian date stew combines the sweetness of dates with the savory taste of meat, creating a unique and delightful flavor. Adjust the quantities based on the number of servings you need.

Khoresht-e Havij Polo Ba Mahicheh

For the Meat Stew (Khoresht-e Havij):

- Stewing meat (lamb or beef), cut into cubes
- Carrots, peeled and sliced
- Onion, finely chopped
- Tomatoes, chopped or tomato paste
- Turmeric, cinnamon, salt, and pepper
- Cooking oil

For the Aromatic Rice (Polo):

- Basmati rice
- Saffron threads (optional, for coloring)
- Butter or cooking oil

Instructions:

Meat Stew (Khoresht-e Havij):

Sauté finely chopped onions in oil until golden.
Add the cubed meat, turmeric, salt, and pepper, browning the meat on all sides.
Stir in chopped tomatoes or tomato paste to create a base for the stew.
Add the sliced carrots to the pot.
Pour in enough water to cover the ingredients, bring to a boil, then reduce heat to simmer.
Sprinkle cinnamon for additional aromatic notes.
Simmer until the meat is tender, and the carrots are cooked through.
Adjust seasoning if needed.

Aromatic Rice (Polo):

Rinse the Basmati rice thoroughly.
In a separate pot, bring water to a boil, add salt, and cook the rice until it's parboiled (half-cooked).
Drain the rice and set aside.
If using saffron, dissolve it in a bit of warm water.
In the pot, layer the partially cooked rice with saffron and butter or oil.
Wrap the pot lid with a clean kitchen towel to absorb steam.

Cook the rice over low heat until it's fully cooked and has developed a crispy layer at the bottom.

Serve Khoresht-e Havij over the aromatic Polo for a delightful combination of meat, carrots, and flavorful rice. Adjust seasoning as needed and enjoy this classic Persian dish!

Khoresht-e Havij Ba Gosht

Ingredients:

- Stewing meat (lamb or beef), cut into cubes
- Carrots, peeled and sliced
- Onion, finely chopped
- Tomatoes, chopped or tomato paste
- Turmeric, cinnamon, salt, and pepper
- Cooking oil

Instructions:

Sauté finely chopped onions in oil until golden.
Add the cubed meat, turmeric, salt, and pepper, browning the meat on all sides.
Stir in chopped tomatoes or tomato paste to create a base for the stew.
Add the sliced carrots to the pot.
Pour in enough water to cover the ingredients, bring to a boil, then reduce heat to simmer.
Sprinkle cinnamon for additional aromatic notes.
Simmer until the meat is tender, and the carrots are cooked through.
Adjust seasoning if needed.

Serve Khoresht-e Havij Ba Gosht over rice or with flatbread. This Persian carrot stew with meat is a flavorful and comforting dish. Adjust the quantities based on the number of servings you need.

Khoresht-e Gheymeh Polo Ba Mahicheh

For the Gheymeh Stew:

- Yellow split peas, soaked and drained
- Stewing meat (lamb or beef), cut into cubes
- Onion, finely chopped
- Tomato paste
- Dried Persian limes (limoo amani), pierced
- Turmeric, salt, and pepper
- Cooking oil

For the Aromatic Rice (Polo):

- Basmati rice
- Saffron threads (optional, for coloring)
- Butter or cooking oil

Instructions:

Gheymeh Stew:

Sauté finely chopped onions in oil until golden.
Add the cubed meat, turmeric, salt, and pepper, browning the meat on all sides.
Stir in tomato paste and continue to sauté.
Add the soaked and drained yellow split peas to the pot.
Pour in enough water to cover the ingredients, bring to a boil, then reduce heat to simmer.
Add the pierced dried Persian limes to the stew for a tangy flavor.
Simmer until the meat is tender, and the split peas are cooked through.
Adjust seasoning if needed.

Aromatic Rice (Polo):

Rinse the Basmati rice thoroughly.
In a separate pot, bring water to a boil, add salt, and cook the rice until it's parboiled (half-cooked).

Drain the rice and set aside.
If using saffron, dissolve it in a bit of warm water.
In the pot, layer the partially cooked rice with saffron and butter or oil.
Wrap the pot lid with a clean kitchen towel to absorb steam.
Cook the rice over low heat until it's fully cooked and has developed a crispy layer at the bottom.

Serve the Gheymeh stew over the aromatic Polo for a classic and delicious Persian dish.

Adjust seasoning as needed.

Khoresht-e Kalam Polo Ba Mahicheh

For the Kalam Stew:

- Stewing meat (lamb or beef), cut into cubes
- Cabbage, chopped
- Onion, finely chopped
- Tomatoes, chopped or tomato paste
- Turmeric, cinnamon, salt, and pepper
- Cooking oil

For the Aromatic Rice (Polo):

- Basmati rice
- Saffron threads (optional, for coloring)
- Butter or cooking oil

Instructions:

Kalam Stew:

Sauté finely chopped onions in oil until golden.
Add the cubed meat, turmeric, salt, and pepper, browning the meat on all sides.
Stir in chopped tomatoes or tomato paste to create a base for the stew.
Add the chopped cabbage to the pot.
Pour in enough water to cover the ingredients, bring to a boil, then reduce heat to simmer.
Sprinkle cinnamon for additional aromatic notes.
Simmer until the meat is tender, and the cabbage is cooked through.
Adjust seasoning if needed.

Aromatic Rice (Polo):

Rinse the Basmati rice thoroughly.
In a separate pot, bring water to a boil, add salt, and cook the rice until it's parboiled (half-cooked).
Drain the rice and set aside.

If using saffron, dissolve it in a bit of warm water.
In the pot, layer the partially cooked rice with saffron and butter or oil.
Wrap the pot lid with a clean kitchen towel to absorb steam.
Cook the rice over low heat until it's fully cooked and has developed a crispy layer at the bottom.

Serve the Kalam stew over the aromatic Polo for a hearty and flavorful Persian dish.

Adjust seasoning as needed.

Khoresht-e Khoresheh

Ingredients:

- Lentils, soaked and drained
- Assorted vegetables (carrots, potatoes, bell peppers), chopped
- Onion, finely chopped
- Tomatoes, chopped or tomato paste
- Turmeric, cumin, coriander, salt, and pepper
- Cooking oil

Instructions:

Sauté finely chopped onions in oil until golden.

Add soaked and drained lentils, turmeric, cumin, coriander, salt, and pepper.

Stir in chopped tomatoes or tomato paste to create a base for the stew.

Add the assorted chopped vegetables to the pot.

Pour in enough water to cover the ingredients, bring to a boil, then reduce heat to simmer.

Simmer until the lentils are cooked through, and the vegetables are tender.

Adjust seasoning if needed.

Serve Khoresht-e Khoresheh over rice or with flatbread. This Persian lentil and vegetable stew provides a nutritious and hearty option. Adjust the quantities based on the number of servings you need.

Khoresht-e Baghali Polo Ba Mahicheh

For the Baghali Polo (Dill Rice):

- Basmati rice
- Fresh dill, chopped
- Lima beans, cooked
- Saffron threads (optional, for coloring)
- Butter or cooking oil
- Salt

For the Mahicheh (Lamb Shank Stew):

- Lamb shanks
- Onion, finely chopped
- Garlic, minced
- Turmeric, cinnamon, salt, and pepper
- Cooking oil

Instructions:

Baghali Polo (Dill Rice):

Rinse the Basmati rice thoroughly.
In a separate pot, bring water to a boil, add salt, and cook the rice until it's parboiled (half-cooked).
Drain the rice and set aside.
Mix the parboiled rice with chopped dill and cooked lima beans.
If using saffron, dissolve it in a bit of warm water and mix it with a portion of the rice.
In a pot, layer the rice and dill mixture with saffron-infused rice.
Add butter or oil between the layers.
Wrap the pot lid with a clean kitchen towel to absorb steam.
Cook the rice over low heat until it's fully cooked and has developed a crispy layer at the bottom.

Mahicheh (Lamb Shank Stew):

Sauté finely chopped onions in oil until golden.
Add lamb shanks, turmeric, salt, and pepper, browning the shanks on all sides.
Stir in minced garlic and sauté for a minute until fragrant.
Add enough water to cover the lamb shanks, bring to a boil, then reduce heat to simmer.
Add cinnamon for additional aromatic notes.
Simmer until the lamb shanks are tender and the stew reaches a desired consistency.
Adjust seasoning if needed.

Serve the Mahicheh over the Baghali Polo for a traditional and flavorful Persian dish.

Adjust seasoning as needed.

Khoresht-e Morgh Polo Ba Mahicheh

For the Morgh Polo (Chicken and Rice):

- Chicken pieces (whole chicken or parts like thighs and drumsticks)
- Basmati rice
- Saffron threads (optional, for coloring)
- Butter or cooking oil
- Salt

For the Mahicheh (Lamb Shank Stew):

- Lamb shanks
- Onion, finely chopped
- Garlic, minced
- Turmeric, cinnamon, salt, and pepper
- Cooking oil

Instructions:

Morgh Polo (Chicken and Rice):

> Rinse the Basmati rice thoroughly.
> In a separate pot, bring water to a boil, add salt, and cook the rice until it's parboiled (half-cooked).
> Drain the rice and set aside.
> In a pot, layer the partially cooked rice with saffron and butter or oil.
> Wrap the pot lid with a clean kitchen towel to absorb steam.
> Cook the rice over low heat until it's fully cooked and has developed a crispy layer at the bottom.
> In a separate pan, brown the chicken pieces in some oil until golden on all sides.

Mahicheh (Lamb Shank Stew):

> Sauté finely chopped onions in oil until golden.
> Add lamb shanks, turmeric, salt, and pepper, browning the shanks on all sides.
> Stir in minced garlic and sauté for a minute until fragrant.

Add enough water to cover the lamb shanks, bring to a boil, then reduce heat to simmer.
Add cinnamon for additional aromatic notes.
Simmer until the lamb shanks are tender and the stew reaches a desired consistency.
Adjust seasoning if needed.

Serve the Mahicheh over the Morgh Polo for a classic and delicious Persian dish. Adjust seasoning as needed.

Khoresht-e Adas Polo Ba Mahicheh

For the Adas Polo (Lentil Rice):

- Basmati rice
- Brown or green lentils, soaked and drained
- Onion, finely chopped
- Raisins (optional)
- Saffron threads (optional, for coloring)
- Butter or cooking oil
- Salt

For the Mahicheh (Lamb Shank Stew):

- Lamb shanks
- Onion, finely chopped
- Garlic, minced
- Turmeric, cinnamon, salt, and pepper
- Cooking oil

Instructions:

Adas Polo (Lentil Rice):

Rinse the Basmati rice thoroughly.
In a separate pot, bring water to a boil, add salt, and cook the rice until it's parboiled (half-cooked).
Drain the rice and set aside.
In a pot, sauté finely chopped onions in oil until golden.
Add the soaked and drained lentils to the pot, sauté briefly.
Mix the parboiled rice with the lentils and onions.
If using saffron, dissolve it in a bit of warm water and mix it with a portion of the rice.
Layer the rice and lentil mixture with saffron-infused rice.
Add butter or oil between the layers.
Optionally, add raisins between the rice layers.
Wrap the pot lid with a clean kitchen towel to absorb steam.

Cook the rice over low heat until it's fully cooked and has developed a crispy layer at the bottom.

Mahicheh (Lamb Shank Stew):

Sauté finely chopped onions in oil until golden.
Add lamb shanks, turmeric, salt, and pepper, browning the shanks on all sides.
Stir in minced garlic and sauté for a minute until fragrant.
Add enough water to cover the lamb shanks, bring to a boil, then reduce heat to simmer.
Add cinnamon for additional aromatic notes.
Simmer until the lamb shanks are tender and the stew reaches a desired consistency.
Adjust seasoning if needed.

Serve the Mahicheh over the Adas Polo for a delightful and hearty Persian dish. Adjust seasoning as needed.

Khoresht-e Loobia Polo Ba Mahicheh

For the Loobia Polo (Green Bean Rice):

- Basmati rice
- Green beans, chopped
- Onion, finely chopped
- Tomato paste
- Turmeric, cinnamon, salt, and pepper
- Cooking oil

For the Mahicheh (Lamb Shank Stew):

- Lamb shanks
- Onion, finely chopped
- Garlic, minced
- Turmeric, cinnamon, salt, and pepper
- Cooking oil

Instructions:

Loobia Polo (Green Bean Rice):

Rinse the Basmati rice thoroughly.
In a separate pot, bring water to a boil, add salt, and cook the rice until it's parboiled (half-cooked).
Drain the rice and set aside.
Sauté finely chopped onions in oil until golden.
Add green beans and sauté briefly.
Stir in tomato paste, turmeric, salt, and pepper to create a base for the rice.
Mix the parboiled rice with the green bean mixture.
Add butter or oil between the layers.
Wrap the pot lid with a clean kitchen towel to absorb steam.
Cook the rice over low heat until it's fully cooked and has developed a crispy layer at the bottom.

Mahicheh (Lamb Shank Stew):

Sauté finely chopped onions in oil until golden.
Add lamb shanks, turmeric, salt, and pepper, browning the shanks on all sides.
Stir in minced garlic and sauté for a minute until fragrant.
Add enough water to cover the lamb shanks, bring to a boil, then reduce heat to simmer.
Add cinnamon for additional aromatic notes.
Simmer until the lamb shanks are tender and the stew reaches a desired consistency.
Adjust seasoning if needed.

Serve the Mahicheh over the Loobia Polo for a delicious and satisfying Persian dish.

Adjust seasoning as needed.

Khoresht-e Zereshk Polo Ba Mahicheh

For the Zereshk Polo (Barberry Rice):

- Basmati rice
- Dried barberries (zereshk), washed and soaked
- Onion, finely chopped
- Saffron threads (optional, for coloring)
- Butter or cooking oil
- Sugar (optional)
- Salt

For the Mahicheh (Lamb Shank Stew):

- Lamb shanks
- Onion, finely chopped
- Garlic, minced
- Turmeric, cinnamon, salt, and pepper
- Cooking oil

Instructions:

Zereshk Polo (Barberry Rice):

>Rinse the Basmati rice thoroughly.
>In a separate pot, bring water to a boil, add salt, and cook the rice until it's parboiled (half-cooked).
>Drain the rice and set aside.
>Sauté finely chopped onions in oil until golden.
>Mix the parboiled rice with the sautéed onions.
>If using saffron, dissolve it in a bit of warm water and mix it with a portion of the rice.
>Layer the rice with saffron-infused rice.
>Add butter or oil between the layers.
>Optionally, sprinkle some sugar over the rice.
>Top the rice with drained and washed dried barberries.
>Wrap the pot lid with a clean kitchen towel to absorb steam.

Cook the rice over low heat until it's fully cooked and has developed a crispy layer at the bottom.

Mahicheh (Lamb Shank Stew):

Sauté finely chopped onions in oil until golden.
Add lamb shanks, turmeric, salt, and pepper, browning the shanks on all sides.
Stir in minced garlic and sauté for a minute until fragrant.
Add enough water to cover the lamb shanks, bring to a boil, then reduce heat to simmer.
Add cinnamon for additional aromatic notes.
Simmer until the lamb shanks are tender and the stew reaches a desired consistency.
Adjust seasoning if needed.

Serve the Mahicheh over the Zereshk Polo for a delightful and aromatic Persian dish.

Adjust seasoning as needed.

Khoresht-e Sib Polo Ba Mahicheh

For the Sib Polo (Apple Rice):

- Basmati rice
- Apples, peeled, cored, and sliced
- Onion, finely chopped
- Saffron threads (optional, for coloring)
- Butter or cooking oil
- Salt

For the Mahicheh (Lamb Shank Stew):

- Lamb shanks
- Onion, finely chopped
- Garlic, minced
- Turmeric, cinnamon, salt, and pepper
- Cooking oil

Instructions:

Sib Polo (Apple Rice):

> Rinse the Basmati rice thoroughly.
> In a separate pot, bring water to a boil, add salt, and cook the rice until it's parboiled (half-cooked).
> Drain the rice and set aside.
> Sauté finely chopped onions in oil until golden.
> Add sliced apples to the sautéed onions and cook until the apples are slightly softened.
> Mix the parboiled rice with the sautéed apples and onions.
> If using saffron, dissolve it in a bit of warm water and mix it with a portion of the rice.
> Layer the rice with saffron-infused rice.
> Add butter or oil between the layers.
> Wrap the pot lid with a clean kitchen towel to absorb steam.
> Cook the rice over low heat until it's fully cooked and has developed a crispy layer at the bottom.

Mahicheh (Lamb Shank Stew):

Sauté finely chopped onions in oil until golden.
Add lamb shanks, turmeric, salt, and pepper, browning the shanks on all sides.
Stir in minced garlic and sauté for a minute until fragrant.
Add enough water to cover the lamb shanks, bring to a boil, then reduce heat to simmer.
Add cinnamon for additional aromatic notes.
Simmer until the lamb shanks are tender and the stew reaches a desired consistency.
Adjust seasoning if needed.

Serve the Mahicheh over the Sib Polo for a sweet and savory Persian dish. Adjust seasoning as needed.